A WATERY WORLD

# TIDES AND CURRENTS

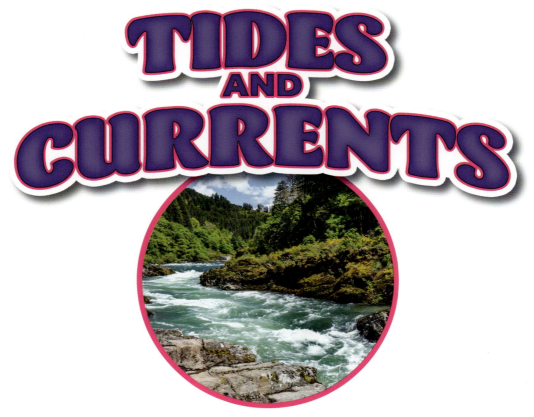

By Emma Carlson Berne
Consultant: Beth Gambro
Reading Specialist, Yorkville, Illinois

Minneapolis, Minnesota

# Teaching Tips

## Before Reading

- Look at the cover of the book. Discuss the picture and the title.
- Ask readers to brainstorm a list of what they already know about tides and currents. What can they expect to see in the book?
- Go on a picture walk, looking through the pictures to discuss vocabulary and make predictions about the text.

## During Reading

- Read for purpose. Encourage readers to think about how water moves as they are reading.
- Ask readers to look for the details of the book. What are they learning about the differences between tides and currents?
- If readers encounter an unknown word, ask them to look at the sounds in the word. Then, ask them to look at the rest of the page. Are there any clues to help them understand?

## After Reading

- Encourage readers to pick a buddy and reread the book together.
- Ask readers to name one thing that causes tides and one that causes currents. Find the pages that tell about these things.
- Ask readers to write or draw something they learned about tides and currents.

**Credits:**

Cover and title page, © amadeustx/Adobe Stock; 3, © Harvepino/iStock; 5, © Nicholas Klein/iStock; 7, © Askolds/iStock; 9, © irisphoto2/iStock 11, © K N/Shutterstock, © Bigmouse108/Shutterstock, © Alfmaler/Shutterstock, and © Studio Barcelona/Shutterstock; 13, © Chris Gordon/iStock; 15T, © KK Stock/Shutterstock; 15B, © mikeledray/Shutterstock; 16–17, © Jaiphet Seehawong/iStock; 19, © SiberianArt/iStock; 21, © CandyRetriever/iStock; 22T, © ShyLama Productions/iStock; 22M, © RainervonBrandis/iStock; 22B, © Grilleau Nicolas/iStock; 23TL, © Michael Hausmann/iStock; 23TM, © simarik/iStock; 23TR, © justinkendra/iStock; 23BL, © JazzIRT/iStock; 23BM, © leolintang/iStock; 23BR, © adisa/iStock.

See BearportPublishing.com for our statement on Generative AI Usage.

Library of Congress Cataloging-in-Publication Data is available at www.loc.gov or upon request from the publisher.

ISBN: 979-8-88916-989-5 (hardcover)
ISBN: 979-8-89232-458-8 (paperback)
ISBN: 979-8-89232-094-8 (ebook)

Copyright © 2025 Bearport Publishing Company. All rights reserved. No part of this publication may be reproduced in whole or in part, stored in any retrieval system, or transmitted in any form or by any means, electronic, mechanical, photocopying, recording, or otherwise, without written permission from the publisher. Bearport Publishing is a division of Chrysalis Education Group.

For more information, write to Bearport Publishing, 5357 Penn Avenue South, Minneapolis, MN 55419.

# Contents

**Water on the Move** . . . . . . . . . . . . . 4

Tides, Currents, and Animals . . . . . . . . . . . . . . 22

Glossary . . . . . . . . . . . . . . . . . . . . . . . . . . . . . . . 23

Index . . . . . . . . . . . . . . . . . . . . . . . . . . . . . . . . . 24

Read More . . . . . . . . . . . . . . . . . . . . . . . . . . . . 24

Learn More Online . . . . . . . . . . . . . . . . . . . . . . 24

About the Author . . . . . . . . . . . . . . . . . . . . . . 24

# Water on the Move

A leaf floats down a stream.

It is going fast in the **current**.

Earth's water is always on the move.

Water goes from one place to another in currents.

Currents move in one **direction**.

Rivers and streams have currents.

The oceans do, too.

What makes this kind of movement?

In rivers, water goes from high places to low places.

Earth's **gravity** is a pull that moves these currents along.

Winds make ocean currents.

Different water **temperatures** do, too.

Cold water **sinks** in the oceans.

Warm water moves in to take its place.

This keeps currents going.

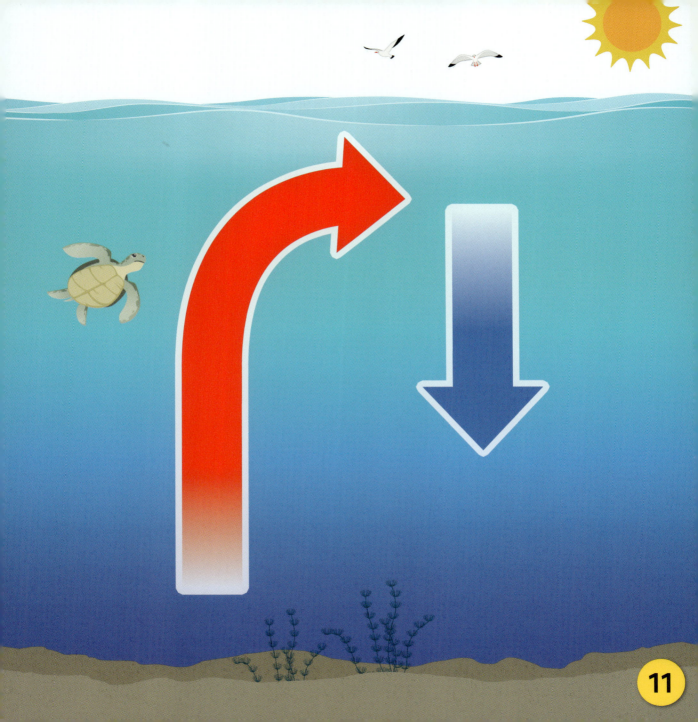

**Tides** are another way ocean water moves.

They push water slowly onto the shore.

Then, they pull it back out into the oceans.

High tide is when the water comes in the most.

It covers more of the land.

When water goes back out, it is low tide.

High tide

Low tide

15

We get tides because of the moon.

Its gravity pulls ocean water.

But its pull is not always felt the same.

Earth spins.

The part facing the moon feels its gravity more.

This pulls water.

It makes high tides.

As Earth spins away, the water goes back down.

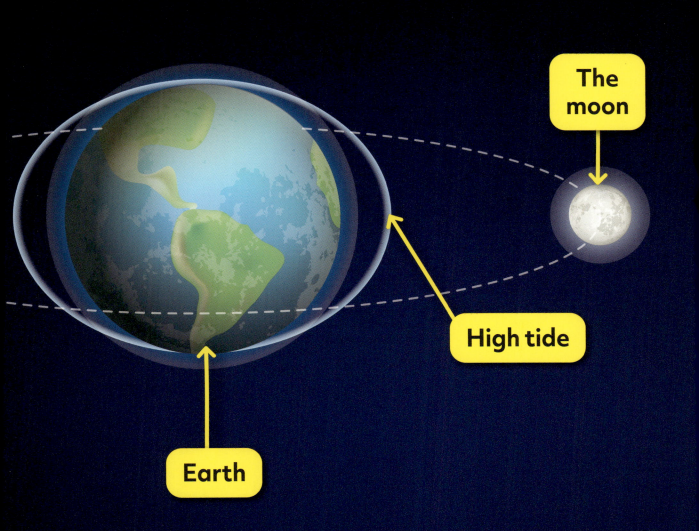

Earth's water is always moving.

It goes from one place to the next.

Dip your toes in.

Can you feel it go?

# Tides, Currents, and Animals

Currents and tides move water. How does this affect water animals?

High tides push sea turtles up the beach. Then, they can lay their eggs in the sand.

Small fish get pulled into deep water during low tide. Bigger fish eat them when this happens.

Many whales swim a long way every year. Ocean currents help these animals get where they need to go.

# Glossary

**current** water always moving in one direction

**direction** the line or course along which something moves

**gravity** a strong pull that moves things

**sinks** moves downward toward the bottom

**temperatures** how hot and cold things are

**tides** movements of water toward and away from shore

## Index

**gravity** 8, 16, 18
**high tide** 14–15, 18–19, 22
**low tide** 14–15, 22
**moon, the** 16, 18–19
**ocean** 6, 10, 12, 16, 22
**river** 6, 8
**shore** 12
**wind** 10

## Read More

**Gaertner, Meg.** *Waves (Science All Around).* Minneapolis: Pop!, 2020.

**Green, Sara.** *Rivers (Our Planet Earth).* Minneapolis: Bellwether Media, 2022.

## Learn More Online

1. Go to **www.factsurfer.com** or scan the QR code below.
2. Enter "**Tides Currents**" into the search box.
3. Click on the cover of this book to see a list of websites.

## About the Author

Emma Carlson Berne lives with her family in Cincinnati, Ohio. She loves splashing in the waves during visits to Florida!